THE HALL OF MOSSES, HOH RAIN FOREST. The temperate rain forests found in the Hoh, Queets, and Quinault River valleys of the park's western side are part of a forest that once stretched up the Pacific Coast of North America from Oregon to Alaska. Dominated by Sitka spruce, western hemlock, Douglas-fir, big-leaf maple, and red alder, these forests are drenched by nearly 14 feet of rain annually. The mild temperatures and extreme precipitation have produced a dense forest and groundcover that includes trillium, oxalis, huckleberry, and mosses as well as liverworts and ferns.

From the WISH YOU WERE HERE® POSTCARD BOOK—Olympic Peninsula

FIRST CLASS POSTAGE REQUIRED

SIERRA PRESS

PHOTO: ©TERRY DONNELLY

RIALTO BEACH, SUNSET. Olympic National Park shelters more than 60 miles of wilderness coastline. The beaches found here are used by gulls, ravens, bald eagles, raccoons, river otters, black bears, and deer. Offshore islands, called seastacks, are protected as wildlife sanctuaries by the National Park Service, the U.S. Fish and Wildlife Service, and the Olympic Coast National Marine Sanctuary. They are important nesting sites for birds that include pelagic cormorants, common murres, rhinoceros auklets, black oystercatchers, and pigeon guillemots.

From the WISH YOU WERE HERE® POSTCARD BOOK—Olympic Peninsula

SIERRA PRESS

PHOTO: ©JAMES RANDKLEV

ELWHA RIVER VALLEY, WINTER. The Elwha River, which empties into the Strait of Juan de Fuca, is one of many rivers that drain the Olympic Peninsula. These rivers provide habitat necessary for the reproduction of five species of salmon as well as steelhead trout. In 1889, the Elwha River Valley was the principal route chosen by an expedition organized by the *Seattle Press* to make the first north-to-south crossing of the peninsula by Euro-Americans. The expedition started in Port Angeles, traveled up the Elwha, and ultimately crossed Low Divide before descending to Lake Quinault on the peninsula's southwest side. It required five-and-a-half months to complete the ordeal.

From the *WISH YOU WERE HERE* POSTCARD BOOK—Olympic Peninsula

SIERRA PRESS

PHOTO: ©PAT O'HARA

SEASTARS AND ANEMONES. The anemones and seastars seen here live in the lower intertidal zone—an ecosystem exposed to air only during the lowest tides. Above this zone lie the middle and upper zones as well as the spray zone which is affected by salt water only during the highest tides or during storms, when heavy salt spray is present. The green sea anemone, which may live hundreds of years, uses its tentacles to sting and immobilize its prey. The prey is then drawn to the center of the anemone, and consumed. Seastars feed not only on anemones, but also include mussels and barnacles in their diet.

From the WISH YOU WERE HERE® POSTCARD BOOK—Olympic Peninsula

SIERRA PRESS

PHOTO: ©PAT O'HARA

SITKA SPRUCE, HOH RAIN FOREST. Sitka spruce is one of the dominant trees found in the temperate rain forests of the Olympic Peninsula's western side. The rain forests once reached from near the coast up the valleys of the Hoh, Queets, and Quinault Rivers. These steep-sided, flat-bottomed valleys receive up to 167 inches of rain annually. Summer precipitation is provided by coastal fog that is funneled up the valleys by prevailing winds, also reducing temperatures. Scientists estimate there are one-million pounds of biological matter per acre here, more than any other ecosystem on Earth.

From the WISH YOU WERE HERE® POSTCARD BOOK—Olympic Peninsula

SIERRA PRESS

PHOTO: ©GEORGE WARD

EVENING LIGHT, LAKE CRESCENT. While Native Americans used Lake Crescent for travel, living, and food Euro-Americans first discovered it in 1849, when John Everett and John Sutherland came across the lake while trapping in the Olympic Mountains. More than 600 feet deep, it was gouged by a lobe of the glacier that flowed through today's Strait of Juan de Fuca during the last major Ice Age. Isolated during and after the ice age, the lake's native populations of rainbow and cutthroat trout gradually evolved into the legendary deep-water Crescenti and Beardslee forms. Found nowhere else on Earth, these are two of the more than 20 types of plants and animals found only on the Olympic Peninsula.

From the *WISH YOU WERE HERE®* POSTCARD BOOK—Olympic Peninsula

SIERRA PRESS

PHOTO: ©PAT O'HARA

NORTHERN SPOTTED OWL. The northern spotted owl lives in the old-growth forests of the Pacific Northwest. Because it often nests in the hollows of snags found here, it is particularly susceptible to the loss of habitat as the result of logging. Many scientists question whether there is enough old-growth forest protected from logging on the Olympic Peninsula to insure its long-term survival here. These forests also provide habitat for the largest unmanaged poulation of Roosevelt elk in the United States (named for President Teddy Roosevelt). In addition, black-tail deer, black bear, river otter, cougar, beaver, and flying squirrel are forest dwellers, as well as the marbled murrelet which—along with the northern spotted owl—is classified as threatened under the Endangered Species Act.

From the WISH YOU WERE HERE• POSTCARD BOOK—Olympic Peninsula

FIRST CLASS POSTAGE REQUIRED

SIERRA PRESS

PHOTO: ©JANIS BURGER

SEASTACK AT SUNSET, SECOND BEACH. The cause of many shipwrecks, the seastacks of the Olympic coast were once part of the coastline but are now isolated by the constant erosive force of pounding surf. Coastal tribes, who have lived on the peninsula for some 12,000 years, once hunted these waters for whales, seals, sea lions, and sea otters from canoes, up to 30 feet in length, carved from the trunks of western redcedar. Today, people of the Hoh, Jamestown Klallam, Lower Elwha Klallam, Makah, Port Gamble Klallam, Skokomish, Quileute, and Quinault cultures continue to live on the peninsula.

From the WISH YOU WERE HERE® POSTCARD BOOK—Olympic Peninsula

SIERRA PRESS

PHOTO: ©JEFF NICHOLAS

WHITE MOUNTAIN SEEN FROM NEAR ANDERSON GLACIER. The mountains of the Olympic Peninsula, which rise nearly 8,000 feet above sea level, are composed of ancient sea-bed sediments (mostly shales and sandstones) and basalts that were formed by volcanic activity on the ancient sea-floor. As the Juan de Fuca Plate, upon which they were originally deposited, came into contact with the North American Plate about 35 million years ago, they were scraped off as the Juan de Fuca Plate plunged under the continental edge. This great mass was folded, fractured, and overturned and has since been eroded by rivers of water and ice into the jumbled, craggy landscape that is found at the center of the peninsula today. More than 600 miles of trails provide access to the great wilderness of mountain, forest, and coast found on the Olympic Peninsula.

From the WISH YOU WERE HERE, POSTCARD BOOK—Olympic Peninsula

SIERRA PRESS

PHOTO: ©PAT O'HARA

SEASTACKS IN FOG, RIALTO BEACH. The waters of the Pacific Ocean, which incessantly pound the western edge of the Olympic Peninsula, support an astonishing diversity of animals. Gulls, ravens, cormorants, and bald eagles patrol the rocks, water, and sky; steelhead trout and five species of salmon migrate seasonally; gray whales regularly cruise offshore waters while orca, blue and humpback whales are more rarely seen; and harbor seals, sea lions, Dall's porpoises, and sea otters are regularly seen in coastal waters.

From the WISH YOU WERE HERE! POSTCARD BOOK—Olympic Peninsula

SIERRA PRESS

PHOTO: ©SHARKSONG/M KAZMERS

MOSS-DRAPED ALDERS, QUINAULT RAIN FOREST. The temperate rain forests of the Olympic Peninsula are home to a tremendous diversity of plant life. More than 250 species of moss thrive in the mild, moist climate. Epiphytes, plants that live on other plants, are represented by 130 species—more species than in any other temperate rain forest in the world. Trees, which may live 200 to 750 years in the rain forest, rise hundreds of feet and are often luxuriantly draped with epiphytes—such as spike-moss and licorice fern—that do no harm, other than occasionally breaking a limb due to their cumulative weight, and often actually nourish their hosts.

From the WISH YOU WERE HERE, POSTCARD BOOK—Olympic Peninsula

SIERRA PRESS

PHOTO: ©TERRY DONNELLY

MOUTH OF KALALOCH CREEK NEAR KALALOCH LODGE.
The creeks and rivers that drain the Olympic Peninsula, in addition to providing spawning grounds for salmon and steelhead, are the source of the veritable forest of driftwood found on many peninsula beaches. Trees washed downstream and out to sea by floodwaters are pounded and smoothed by surf and the rocky shoreline. High tides caused by storms later deposit them on the beach above the normal high tide line. The footprints of bear, deer, river otter, raccoon, ravens, gulls, and beachcombers regularly intermingle in this jumble of fallen, bleached trees.

From the WISH YOU WERE HERE! POSTCARD BOOK—Olympic Peninsula

SIERRA PRESS

PHOTO: ©TERRY DONNELLY

SOL DUC FALLS, SOL DUC RIVER. The lowland forest, which borders the Sol Duc ("sparkling waters"), is one of four forest types found on the Olympic Peninsula. The lowland, which is found inland from the coast and in areas drier than the coast's temperate rain forests, is dominated by western hemlock, Douglas-fir, and western redcedar. Rope, capes, skirts, aprons, mats, and baskets were fashioned from the stringy bark of the redcedar and canoes, up to 30 feet in length, were carved from whole trees by the native peoples of the Olympic Peninsula. These traditional canoes continue to be made today and are used for work, pleasure, and sport.

from the WISH YOU WERE HERE® POSTCARD BOOK —Olympic Peninsula

SIERRA PRESS

PHOTO: ©STEVE TERRILL

HURRICANE RIDGE, WINTER. The Olympic Mountains, which rise nearly 8,000 feet above sea level, create a great barrier to moisture-laden air masses approaching North America from the Pacific Ocean. Forced upward by the mountains, these air masses are cooled and forced to release their moisture as either rain or, higher up in the mountains, snow. The Olympics are so successful at wringing moisture from these storms that they create a "rain shadow." The western slopes of the Olympics receive more than 220 inches of precipitation per year while in Sequim—on the northeast side of the peninsula only 34 miles from Mount Olympus—barely 18 inches of rain falls.

From the WISH YOU WERE HERE ■ POSTCARD BOOK—Olympic Peninsula

SIERRA PRESS

PHOTO: ©PAT O'HARA